AWESOME ANIMALS IN THEIR HABITATS

PROTECTING BACKYARD ANIMALS

PAIGE V. POLINSKY

Consulting Editor, Diane Craig, M.A./Reading Specialist

Sandcastle

An Imprint of Abdo Publishing
abdopublishing.com

abdopublishing.com

Published by Abdo Publishing, a division of ABDO, PO Box 398166, Minneapolis, Minnesota 55439. Copyright © 2017 by Abdo Consulting Group, Inc. International copyrights reserved in all countries. No part of this book may be reproduced in any form without written permission from the publisher. SandCastle™ is a trademark and logo of Abdo Publishing.

Printed in the United States of America, North Mankato, Minnesota

102016
012017

THIS BOOK CONTAINS
RECYCLED MATERIALS

Editor: Rebecca Felix
Content Developer: Nancy Tuminelly
Cover and Interior Design and Production: Mighty Media, Inc.
Photo Credits: Allen Birnbach/Cesar's Way Inc., iStockphoto, Shutterstock Images

Publisher's Cataloging-in-Publication Data

Names: Polinsky, Paige V., author.
Title: Protecting backyard animals / by Paige V. Polinsky.
Description: Minneapolis, MN : Abdo Publishing, 2017. | Series: Awesome animals in their habitats
Identifiers: LCCN 2016944676 | ISBN 9781680784251 (lib. bdg.) | ISBN 9781680797787 (ebook)
Subjects: LCSH: Animals--Habitations--Juvenile literature. | Habitat (Ecology)--Juvenile literature. | Wildlife conservation--Juvenile literature.
Classification: DDC 577--dc23
LC record available at http://lccn.loc.gov/2016944676

SandCastle™ Level: Transitional

SandCastle™ books are created by a team of professional educators, reading specialists, and content developers around five essential components—phonemic awareness, phonics, vocabulary, text comprehension, and fluency—to assist young readers as they develop reading skills and strategies and increase their general knowledge. All books are written, reviewed, and leveled for guided reading, early reading intervention, and Accelerated Reader™ programs for use in shared, guided, and independent reading and writing activities to support a balanced approach to literacy instruction. The SandCastle™ series has four levels that correspond to early literacy development. The levels are provided to help teachers and parents select appropriate books for young readers.

EMERGING · BEGINNING · TRANSITIONAL · FLUENT

CONTENTS

ABOUT BACKYARDS

Backyards can be many sizes. They are found in all **climates**.

Backyards are home to many animals.

Some backyard animals are hard
to see.

Worms live **underground**. Some
mice do too.

Most birds live in trees.

So do some bats. Bats sleep during
the day. At night, they eat **insects**.

Butterflies live in backyards.

Bees do too. These **insects** both
need flowers for food.

Rabbits live in backyards.

So do squirrels. Squirrels eat
acorns.

Dogs play in backyards.

Cesar Millan is a dog **behaviorist**. He teaches people how to care for their dogs.

Humans cut down trees to build houses. Many backyard animals lose their homes this way.

Pesticides can hurt those that stay.

Backyards give food and shelter to many animals. And these animals help us in return.

Bees and butterflies carry **pollen** between flowers. This helps new plants grow.

You can help make backyards safe
for animals! Make a bird feeder.

Plant a flower garden. And never
use **pesticides** in your yard.

THINK ABOUT IT

Have you ever played in a backyard?
What animals did you see there?

GLOSSARY

acorn – the seed of an oak tree.

behaviorist – a person who studies animal behaviors.

climate – the weather and temperatures that are normal in a certain place.

insect – a small animal that has six legs and three main parts to its body.

pesticide – something used to destroy pests, especially bugs.

pollen – the fine powder found in flowers.

underground – below the surface of the earth.